CONTENTS

STAYING SAFE ONLINE
It's always best to check with a parent or guardian before playing online with others.

LittleBrother
B O O K S

Published 2022.
Little Brother Books Ltd, Ground Floor, 23 Southernhay East, Exeter, Devon EX1 1QL
Printed in the United Kingdom.
books@littlebrotherbooks.co.uk | www.littlebrotherbooks.co.uk

SPENDING ROBUX
Buying items in the game costs Robux, so check with an adult first before purchasing content.

WELCOME TO THE ROBLOX UNIVERSE

Roblox is packed with hours of fun, including all kinds of awesome online games, character customisation and even the ability to make your own video games!

CUSTOMISED AVATAR

If you're new to the world of Roblox, then you'll want to start by creating your own avatar. Choose from different faces, hair, clothing, pets and more.

Currently Wearing

3D

Friends (1)

See All →

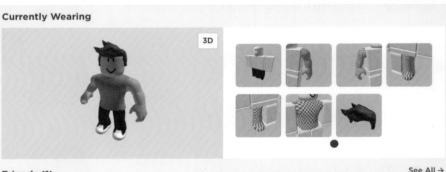

Most Engaging

[UPD 21] Anime Fighters
👍93% 👤42K

Bee Swarm Simulator
👍94% 👤39.1K

[Trials of 200] Mighty Omega
👍87% 👤628

[🔥x2] Anime Punching
👍92% 👤2.5K

NEW BOSS! Anime Fighting
👍94% 👤9.5K

🐉[Cyber City] Giant Simulator
👍94% 👤5K

[🗡x2 Luck🗡] Sword Factory
👍89% 👤4.2K

[UPD7] ⚔ Clicker Simulator!⚔
👍95% 👤25.2K

⭐ Super Power Training
👍73% 👤1.8K

Recommended For You

Brookhaven 🏡 RP
👍86% 👤364.3K

[❤ Axolotls!] Pet Simulator X!
👍93% 👤102.5K

[UPD7] ⚔ Clicker Simulator!
👍95% 👤25.2K

[🎃 UPDATE 17] Blox Fruits
👍93% 👤143.6K

Adopt Me!
👍83% 👤146.9K

[UPD4.1+2x⚔💰] Weapon Fighting
👍94% 👤24.5K

Find the Markers (151)
👍83% 👤45.2K

Livetopia🏡 New house!
👍81% 👤60.5K

Build A Boat For Treasure
👍92% 👤46.6K

ROBLOX EXPERIENCES

There are so many Roblox games to play, that you'll never get bored. Choose from all kinds of experiences, such as RPGs, adventure, sports and simulators.

SPENDING ROBUX

Although there are plenty of free Roblox games to try, some require you to spend Robux. Find out all about how to buy and earn this in-game currency on page 8.

Buy Robux

Get Robux to purchase upgrades for your avatar or buy special abilities in experiences. For more information on how to earn Robux, visit our **Robux Help page**.
Purchase Roblox Premium to get more Robux for the same price. Roblox Premium is billed every month until cancelled. **Learn more here.**

	Buy Robux	Subscribe and get more!
£4.59	◎ 400	◎ 450/month
£8.99	◎ 800	◎ 1,000/month

SOLO GAMING

The best way to become a Roblox pro is to try out lots of games. Start off on your own and explore the many different types of experiences on offer.

ONLINE ACTION

Once you've figured out which Roblox games you really like, join other players online for even more fun. Send your friends invitations and they can join in too!

ROBLOX YOUTUBERS

One of the best ways to improve your Roblox skills is to watch other players at work. Check out our list of the best Roblox YouTubers to watch on page 32.

ROBLOX STUDIO

If you've ever wanted to try making your own video games, then Roblox is a great place to start. Sign up for Roblox Studio and see what cool stuff you can create.

This Ultimate Guide is packed full of Roblox tips, secrets, top 10 lists and much more. Inside you'll discover everything you need to know to become a Roblox pro gamer!

WHAT'S NEW IN ROBLOX

The Roblox universe is always evolving and changing, with fun games to play, creators sharing their ideas and cool events taking place. Here's what's new!

PLAY VR GAMES

If you have a VR headset, you can play all kinds of cool Roblox VR games. Check out Cleaning Simulator, VRBLOX, Sound Space, Koala Café, Laser Tag VR and more.

BUY OFFSALE ITEMS

Players can purchase items no longer available in the online store. Rare offsale items can be traded or bought using Robux, but they might cost a lot.

BIG MONEY

Did you know that Roblox developers and creators earned more than £500 million in 2021 by making games and selling items? That's massive!

LIVE EVENTS

There have been all sorts of amazing live events on Roblox recently. These have included concerts, the Annual Bloxy Awards, a treasure hunt and more.

VISIT NIKELAND

In 2021 Nike and Roblox teamed up to create a very cool world. NIKELAND includes game to play, the ability to design your own games and even a digital showroom.

CHAT WITH FRIENDS

Although spatial voice chat has been added to Roblox, only players who are over 13 years-old can currently use the new feature.

HIGH FASHION

World famous designer fashion house Ralph Lauren has started selling digital clothing in Roblox. Items cost between 125 to 300 Robux each.

CHIPOTLE HALLOWEEN

Mexican fast food chain Chipotle hosted a spooky Halloween event in 2021. The first 30,000 players to visit its virtual location in Roblox got a free burrito in real life!

TOP 10

ROBLOX GAMES FOR BEGINNERS

If you're just starting to explore the world of Roblox, here are 10 great games that are perfect for beginners to try out!

1

TROPICAL RESORT TYCOON

This is a game that lets players build their very own hotels, villa and resorts on a tropical island. You can also have lots of fun exploring the island online with friends.

2

JAILBREAK

Take on the role of either a guard or an inmate at a maximum-security prison and either try to break out successfully or stop everyone from escaping from the jail!

3

WELCOME TO BLOXBURG

Take a look at this open-world simulation set in a Roblox-style city. You can get a job, earn money, buy a house and make new friends – this game has it all.

4

ADOPT ME!

If you've ever wanted to raise and take care of a cute pet, here's your chance. This is an easy game to pick up and play with friends, plus it gets lot of updates.

5

SPEED RUN 4

One of the best obstacle course games (or obbys) in Roblox, Speed Run 4 has over 31 levels to tackle. Can you make it to the finish line without falling off the edge?

6

MEEPCITY

Take a trip to MeepCity and play all sorts of fun games! Earn coins by trying different games and then use them to buy items to customise your own house.

7

SUPER HERO TYCOON

Now you can become a superhero and build a cool base. Play as Spider-Man, Batman, The Flash, Ant-Man, The Hulk and many other comic book characters.

8

WORK AT A PIZZA PLACE

The only problem with this game is that it will make you really hungry! Learn to manage a pizza shop, make deliveries and earn cash to buy all sorts of upgrades.

9

BOOOA BOOGA

Play together in a tribe and try to survive the many challenges on a number of island worlds. Fight off enemies, gather resources and work together to level up.

10

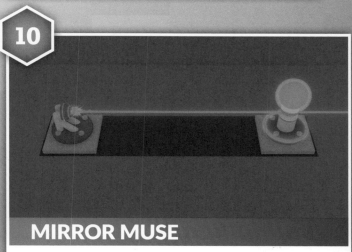

MIRROR MUSE

This is a unique one-player game that includes over 50 tricky puzzles to try. Each one uses mirrors and lasers, so you'll need very quick reflexes to beat them!

CATALOG AND ROBLOX

To customise your character and buy all sorts of cool goodies, just head on over to the Avatar Shop. Here you can start spending Robux, which is the in-game currency.

Midnight Blue Fang Face Mask
By BlizYror
50

Bow Purse - Black
By @Mimi_Dev
100

Radioactive Purse (1.0)
By @Joylessly
60

Cat Belty Pack V1
By @Sofioann
25

Pink Peppermint Purse
By @CodyDevv
45

Woman Punk Funny Pack
By @Sofioann
45

Glamorous Gothic Green
By @Martin_Rblx2
100

Mooncat Purse Red
By @Martin_Rblx2
75

Eternal Heart Pin
300

Miau Chocolate Purse 3.0 White
By @cyaleys
60

There are all kinds of free items in the Avatar Shop that are worth getting. However, a lot of the best items require you to spend Robux in order to add them to your inventory.

To make your avatar look unique, it's possible to try on items before you buy them. You can check out your character from any angle and even in 3D. What outfits are you going to wear today?

Silly Fun
Free

Golden Headphones -
Free

Junkbot
Free

True Blue Hair
Free

Linlin
Free

Rthro Animation Package
Free

Orange Beanie with Black Hair
Free

Lavender Updo
Free

Happy New Year Rat
Free

The Winning Smile
Free

Blue Namahage Mask
By @Guestdere

Price	85
	Buy
Type	Accessory | Face
Genres	All
Updated	Jul 02, 2021
Description	Red version: https://www.roblox.com/catalog/7037890272/Red-Namahage-Mask
	Read More

Take Off | 3D

It's possible to swap your avatar's face, body, arms, legs, hair, clothing and emote as many times as you like. There are also lots of accessories to be picked up that can really make your character one-of-a-kind.

528

You can buy Robux in the game itself or pick up Roblox Gift Cards from shops in real life. If you go for a Card, you can also get exclusive virtual items that aren't available anywhere else.

Digital Gift Card £25

ROBLOX

2,000 Robux

Get one of these exclusive virtual items when you redeem a Roblox Gift Card!

| New Year's Clock Pal £10 Gift Card | New Year's Confetti Popper Hat £25 Gift Card | New Year's Celebration Hat £50 Gift Card | New Year's Countdown Hat £100 Gift Card |

2,040

2,040 Robux

Buy Robux

Buy Robux

Get Robux to purchase upgrades for your avatar or buy special abilities in games. For more information on how to earn Robux, visit our Robux Help page. Purchase Roblox Premium to get more Robux for the same price. Roblox Premium is billed every month until cancelled. Learn more here.

Buy Robux   Subscribe and get more!

Keep an eye on your Robux balance shown at the top of the screen. As you purchase items from the Avatar Shop, the balance will go down. Once you've spent all of your Robux, you'll need to buy some more.

Earn more Robux by creating and selling custom items to other players. For every item you sell you'll be paid in Robux, which can then be put towards buying even more stuff from the Avatar Shop.

Buy Robux™

R$

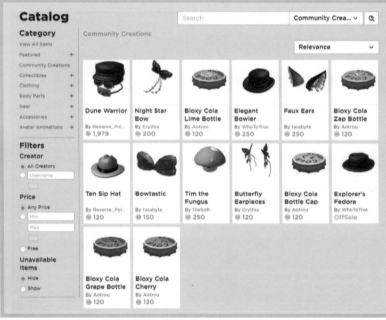

Catalog

Search   Community Crea... ▾ 🔍

Category
View All Items
Featured   +
Community Creations
Collectibles   +
Clothing   +
Body Parts   +
Gear   +
Accessories   +
Avatar Animations   +

Community Creations   Relevance ▾

| Dune Warrior By Reverse_Pol... ⏣ 1,979 | Night Star Bow By Erythia ⏣ 200 | Bloxy Cola Lime Bottle By Aotrou ⏣ 120 | Elegant Bowler By WhoToTrus ⏣ 250 | Faux Ears By tarabyte ⏣ 250 | Bloxy Cola Zap Bottle By Aotrou ⏣ 120 |

Filters
Creator
◉ All Creators
○ Username
Go

Price
◉ Any Price
○ Min
○ Max
Go
○ Free

Unavailable Items
◉ Hide
○ Show

| Ten Sip Hat By Reverse_Pol... ⏣ 120 | Bowtastic By tarabyte ⏣ 150 | Tim the Fungus By DieSoft ⏣ 250 | Butterfly Earpieces By Erythia ⏣ 120 | Bloxy Cola Bottle Cap By Aotrou ⏣ 120 | Explorer's Fedora By WhoToTrus OffSale |
| Bloxy Cola Grape Bottle By Aotrou ⏣ 120 | Bloxy Cola Cherry By Aotrou ⏣ 120 | | | | |

Dedicated fans can also sign up for Roblox Premium, a paid-for subscription service that includes a monthly Robux allowance. Members can get access to exclusive items and trade with other players.

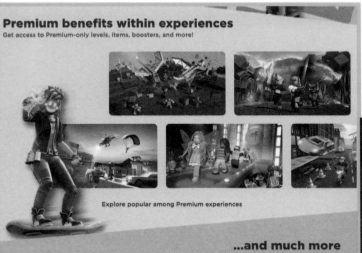

Premium benefits within experiences
Get access to Premium-only levels, items, boosters, and more!

Explore popular among Premium experiences

...and much more

ROBLOX

PREMIUM

BEST

There are plenty of amazing Roblox adventure games to try, but here's a selection of some of the best that are really worth trying out!

ADVENTURE GAMES

BUILD A BOAT FOR TREASURE

Some of the best Roblox games are often the simplest. In Build a Boat For Treasure, players have to make their own water-based craft using a limited budget. If built successfully, you'll pass on to the next region.

Whilst this may sound easy enough, each level is filled with all kinds of obstacles to avoid such as barricades in the water and even rivers of lava. Make it to the end safely to find the secret treasure.

Join the Build a Boat For Treasure group and you'll receive 25% more gold, 300% more health, +4 barrels of TNT and much more. Start building your boat today and get ready to set sail!

ROBOT 64

This game owes a lot to the legendary Mario 64, but it's also a great 3D platformer in its own right. Players take on the role of Beebo, a small robot who's helping his master to destroy the sun by throwing ice cream at it!

Run, jump and explore a huge world, battling a variety of enemies and taking on big boss battles. It's also possible to travel further and faster with the aid of a handy jetpack accessory.

The controls of Robot 64 are spot-on and the game's wacky worlds are filled with all sorts of things that will put a smile on your face. Over 41 million players have visited Robot 64, so go try it for yourself.

There are a number of remote islands to explore in the game, each of which has secrets to uncover and challenges to be undertaken. With the right ship, weapons and skills you'll become an expert plunderer in no time.

The game has proven to be so popular that it's possible to pick up Roblox: A Pirate's Tale action figures too. Each two-pack includes a code to download an exclusive virtual item to use in the game. Yaaaar!

A PIRATE'S TALE

Set in the world of the Cursed Seas, A Pirate's Tale is an open-world game that lets you live the life of a notorious buccaneer. Travel across the ocean, search for buried treasure and battle fearsome foes.

HIDE AND SEEK EXTREME

If you're looking for a Roblox game to keep you on your toes, then this might be the one. In Hide and Seek Extreme players choose a random map and decide who will be the seeker and who will be hiding.

The levels are massive and there are all sorts of places to sneak off to, but if you move around too much you may be spotted. The seeker also only has a limited amount of time to find everyone before it's game over.

In addition, the seeker can access a number of special abilities such as Glue, Camera, Sprint and Stun that can help them find hiders.

Once the seeker has managed to find everyone, it's game over and you can all swap roles and start again.

SCUBA DIVING AT QUILL LAKE

A bit of hidden gem, this is one Roblox game that's worth searching for. This is a scuba diving adventure that takes place in a huge lake that has all sorts of mysteries waiting to be uncovered.

The underwater world looks incredible and there is so much to see and do when submerged. The game is also quite peaceful and you can take your time exploring without worrying about being attacked.

There are a number of water-based minigames in the shape of Seaside Challenges. See if you can find over 100 artifacts hidden in the lake and you'll be playing Scuba Diving at Quill Lake for quite a while.

LITTLE WORLD

This is one of the coolest Roblox games currently available. Begin your journey as a cute little ladybird and try to survive whatever nature throws at you. Collect fruit, train and explore to evolve into other creatures.

Little World is a grand survival game mixed with a dash of arcade action that's really fun to experience. See if you can make it to the very top of the food chain and become the game's ultimate apex predator!

It's actually possible to level up infinitely and try tackling the global leaderboards. New species, evolutions and challenges are added regularly, so you'll definitely want to check out Little World.

ISLANDS

Similar in appearance to Minecraft, this blocky adventure game lets players build their own island, create huge farms, raise animals and more. You'll need to collect resources, craft items and defeat bosses too.

Islands can be played on your own, or you can always team up with other players to explore the world and take on challenges together. Regular updates to the game mean that there's always something new to see and do.

There are even special events taking place in the world, such as the recent Lunar New Year theme. So if you're a fan of Minecraft who's looking for something similar to try, Islands is well-worth your time.

THE LABYRINTH

Here's a semi-spooky game that you might just want to play with the lights on! A puzzle adventure, The Labyrinth challenges players to find their way through a tricky maze in one piece.

These can be tackled on your own or by teaming up with others to solve each mazes mysteries. Each level features creepy noises and a chilling atmosphere, which really adds to the game's suspense.

Players can find all sorts of resources to craft tools and weapons to help them, with a PvP mode that lets you duel it out to see who's the best. The game has had over 48 million visits and certainly earns its spot on this list.

THE SHARK HAS BEEN RELEASED

SHARK BITE

This is a great game that can be really fun to play with your friends! In Shark Bite you either take on the role of the hunter of the deep or be on a boat which the shark is trying to destroy. Which of you will survive?

Whilst you'd think the answer would be obvious, the players on the boat are armed with a variety of weapons with which to defend themselves.

If they manage to survive a round, they'll then make it through to the next one.

Of course, playing as the shark is also lots of fun too, as you can sneak up on players when they least expect it. Jump out of the water and take a big bite out of their boat before diving back into the sea. It's awesome!

DRAGON ADVENTURES

If it's a truly epic multiplayer experience you're after, then Dragon Adventures has it all. With a vast open-world map, travel across the land in search of a variety of dragons to help you protect your fortress.

The game is loads of fun when you team up with your friends either to work together and battle enemies or to try and destroy each other's fortresses. It's even possible to design your own base.

Dragon Adventures receives regular updates and all-new Bossfights were added in 2021. Find dragon eggs, raise your creatures, grow crops to feed them and take to the air and explore the kingdom.

THE WILD WEST

With over 158 million views, The Wild West is a hugely successful Roblox title. Players find themselves dropped into a town in the middle of the desert and have to fight off all sorts of outlaws and crooks.

It's possible to choose from either a hero or villain character to complete quests, robberies and a variety of missions. Finish tasks to earn lots of money and buy new outfits, accessories, horses and weapons.

There's so much to see and do in the Old West, that you'll never get bored. Whether you're robbing the Bronze City stage or hunting down bounties for the sheriff, there's something here for everyone.

ROYALE HIGH

One of the biggest Roblox games to date, Royale High has been visited over 6 billion times! The game has a very loyal fanbase that enjoys exploring the world, playing fun games, uncovering secrets and earning currency to upgrade their characters.

In the ever-growing dream world of Royale High, players can travel around a magical fantasy land using a Teleportation Sceptre. By taking part in challenges, you'll earn Diamonds, which can then be spent on special items, clothing and abilities.

Players can also level up by attending lessons at Royale High School classes. The higher the grades you get, the more rewards you'll earn. With so much to see and do, this is one Roblox game that you'll come back to time and again!

ROBLOX

TOP 10

FAVOURITED AVATAR ITEMS

You can buy all sorts of amazing items from the Roblox Avatar Shop and use them to customise your character. Check out this list of the top 10 favourited items in the Shop, as voted for by players from around the world!

1 EXCLUSIVE LIGHTNING ADIDAS JACKET GREEN: 25 ROBUX

This great jacket from Eclipse Clothing is a snazzy green colour, with a white adidas T-shirt underneath. This item has had over 1.5 million likes in the Avatar Shop!

2 ONLY PEOPLE WITH BIG ROUX CAN WEAR IT: 2 ROBUX

Costing just two Robux, this plain white T-shirt features a fiery logo that shows how much of a Roblox fan you are. Over 680,000 players have given this item the thumbs-up.

3 SUPER SUPER HAPPY FACE: 113,999 ROBUX

Add the Super Super Happy Face to your character and you'll be as pleased as the 1.1 million players who have added it to their favourites lists.

4 VALKYRIE HELM: 260,000 ROBUX

The description of this pricey item states that it's a replica of a helm worn by the Valkyries, a group of fearsome female warriors who serve mighty Odin.

5 FROM THE VAULT: DOZENS OF DINOSAURS: 7,999 ROBUX

This limited-time item costs just short of 8,000 Robux, but that's a small price to pay for Sharksie's pack of 14 plushie dinos for you to enjoy!

6 TRUE BLUE HAIR: FREE

A simple Avatar item, but one that's been favourited more than 1.6 million times. This accessory will definitely give your character a very unique look.

7 BEAR FACE MASK: 100 ROBUX

Stay safe and cute with this fun Bear Mask! This accessory only costs 100 Robux, so is a very affordable item to add to your character's inventory.

8 HAPPY NEW YEAR RAT: FREE

We might be well into 2022, but there's still time to celebrate with the Happy New Year Rat. This cute mammal is the first sign from the Chinese Zodiac.

9 CURSED FLAMES: 50 ROBUX

Add these fiery floaters to your character and players will wonder just what you've done to make Cursed Flames follow you around!

10 WOMAN: FREE

The companion to its Man counterpart, this bundle has been favourited over three million times, which is pretty amazing even for a free Roblox item!

BEST RPGs

RPG WORLD

First released in 2019, RPG World has since had over 50 million visits. There are usually a few hundred players online at all times, so there are plenty of chances to team-up.

The aim of the game is very easy. Hunt down and destroy lots of monsters, level up and get new gear. Keep repeating this pattern and you'll soon be a formidable warrior!

Players can also buy lots of different pets to help them unlock new areas of the world. Use the code 'joined' when joining the Crackin' Games Group to get 500 free crystals.

LEGEND RPG 2

This is a great RPG that's packed with all sorts of cool of things to do. In Legend RPG 2, players have to battle fearsome enemies, clear challenging dungeons, level up and buy lots of new items.

The game has a great anime feel, so looks really unique. There are lots of different characters in the game too, so it's fun discovering and battling them all.

A special limited time Winter Dungeon even dropped in 2021 and included special weapons, armour and other exclusive items that players could collect.

The game gets lots of regular updates including new EXP rewards, upgraded spells and items. Form a party or guild and battle bosses as a team!

VESTERIA

Not only one of the best Roblox games, let alone RPGs available, Vesteria is truly epic. Explore a vast world full of characters, adventures and hidden treasures.

Whilst most of the game is free, there are some parts of it that will cost you Robux to access, but it's definitely worth parting with your loot to open them up.

KNIGHT SIMULATOR

If it's a truly massive RPG that you're after, then Knight Simulator is the one for you. Released in 2020, the game has had over three million visits and more each day.

As well as a huge world to explore, there are over 230 different weapons to collect and nearly 100 different suits of armour available to add to your own collection.

Trade with other players to get special items, discover hidden silver and golden chests, rank up, climb the leader board and then enter new worlds!

FANTASTIC FRONTIER

In Fantastic Frontier you get to travel to a variety of unique islands that each have their own challenges, plus there's always something new to see and do.

Fight all kinds of monsters, collect rare items, weapons and armour, fish, hunt birds and more. Use loot to upgrade your character, weapons and home.

The Spring 2022 update added a huge new island to wander around, with even more weapons, armour, buildings and quests. Just purchase the Boathouse to access it.

RPG SIMULATOR

This game has been created by Astral Studios and has clocked up a whopping 110 million visits to date. This is one truly massive RPG that has to be seen to be believed.

Players can battle through a number of realms on their own, or team up with others to tackle sneaky enemies, tough bosses and tricky quests.

Obtain the very best loot by fighting in Raids and Zones. Be sure to buy yourself a pet too, as companions can really help you out in battles.

ROCITIZENS

Instead of a classic fantasy world, RoCitizens is set in a modern city. Get a job, complete quests for the local people, furnish a home and chat to other players.

RoCitizens was created in 2013 and had over 750 million visits. Players like to pop in regularly to see what's new and what game updates there have been.

There are seasonal events in the game too, including Christmas, Halloween to Spring Break-themed adventures. Just watch out for any criminals on the loose!

SUNDOWN ISLAND

Why play an RPG as a human being when you can adventure as an animal? In Sundown Island you take on the role of a wolf trying to survive in a strange land.

There are dangers lurking around every corner, so be sure to customise your wolf with different accessories before heading off on an adventure.

Join a pack to make new friends and explore the misty world as a team. From snowy landscapes to enchanted forests, Sundown Island really does have it all.

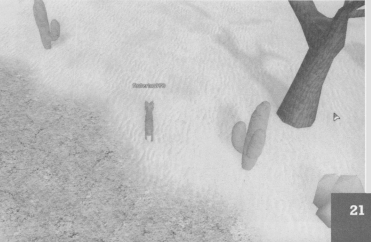

NOMRIAL LEGENDS

If you're an experienced RPG player, then Nomrial Legends is the game for you. It features epic quests, mythical weapons and very tough monsters to battle.

Although the world in the game might not be as large as those in other Roblox RPGs, it's still packed with details, features, enemies and a cool story just waiting to be discovered.

Train hard, level up, equip the best weapons, armour and equipment that you have, then set off on an adventure to free the land of the evil Lord Ultimus!

SWORDBURST 2

Although you can play through Swordburst 2 on your own, this is definitely one Roblox RPG that's tons more fun when you join a group of other warriors.

The world in this game is massive. There's always something new to discover, but you'll need to beat bosses before you can unlock each area.

There are many rare items to be found throughout Swordburst 2, so you'll need to fully explore each area of the world to locate them all.

PORTAL HEROES

A remake of a much older Roblox game, Portal Heroes takes place in a fantasy world connected by portals. Jump through each gateway to access a new area.

Carefully choose your weapons, armour and accessories before heading off into battle against tough enemies. Win a fight to collect gold coins.

Portal Heroes is also quite a funny game for an RPG. One of the boss characters is a tiny rubber duck that's actually an evil monster. Argh!

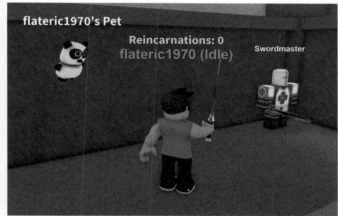

INFINITY RPG

A lot of RPGs require you to do plenty of grinding in order to level up. The same is true of Infinity RPG, which has 50 different fantasy worlds to explore.

Fight monsters, collect over 400 weapons and blast enemies with magical spells. This is one RPG that will take you many, many hours to fully complete.

There's so much to see and do in Infinity RPG, from unlocking over 70 sets of armour to exploring three universal dimensions. This is one truly epic Roblox RPG!

ROBLOX

TOP 10

TIPS, TRICKS AND SECRETS

The Roblox universe is packed full of tips, tricks and secrets just waiting to be discovered. How many of these hidden treats have you discovered?

1

ROBLOX LAUNDROMAT

Play Roblox Laundromat and you can earn yourself a secret badge! The badge can be found hidden in a green van parked outside the Walmart store.

2

BROOKHAVEN

In Brookhaven, enter the Auto Shop, pass by the counter into the room and click the mop set on the right. A door behind it leads to a secret criminal base.

3

ADOPT ME

To find eight secret obbies in Adopt Me, go to the playground on Adoption Island. Look behind the slide to find a small building with an 'obbies' sign.

4

BEDWARS

From the main multiplayer hub in BedWars, head passed the pink 'islands' door and then drop off the edge of the map to find a secret lava-filled cave.

5

MEEPCITY

There are two secret rooms in MeepCity's school. Head through the vent in the basement to check out the hidden teacher's lounge and gaming hideout.

6

ADVENTURE STORY

Select Mellow Meadows in Adventure Story and then find a door behind a large block. Complete two obbies to get a tasty hoagie sandwich. Yum, yum!

7

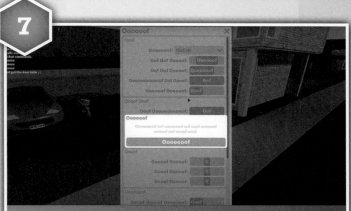

WELCOME TO BLOXBURG

Did you know you can actually change the languages in Welcome to Bloxburg by going to the Options menu and selecting either Robonese or Oofish?

8

ROCITIZENS

Head to the river near the bridge in RoCitizens and find a bit of wall that has a different texture. Swim to the end of the tunnel to find a secret hidden room.

9

VESTERIA

In Vesteria, head to the mushroom forest and find a group of large mushrooms in a hole. Bounce on them up to a treehouse containing a free mushroom hat.

10

ROBLOX HIGH SCHOOL 2

Go to Madi's hideout on the weekend in Roblox High School 2, buy the school basement key. Try all the doors to find one with a golden treasure chest.

BEST ACTION GAMES

There are plenty of amazing Roblox adventure games to try, but here's a selection of some of the best that are really worth trying out!

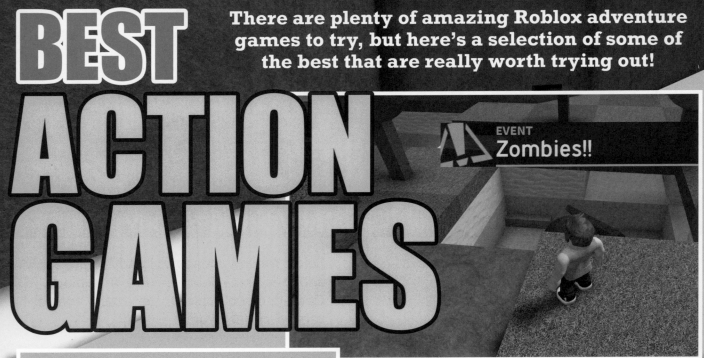

SUPER BOMB SURVIVAL

You'll need fast reflexes to make it out of this game in one piece. The aim of Super Bomb Survival is to dodge a variety of dangerous objects dropping from the sky.

These can include dynamite on a timer and flames that spread around you. Explosions also damage the level you're on, giving you less places to hide.

Each round lasts two-and-a-half minutes and it's usually a mad scramble to avoid getting blown up. Try this game solo and then with your friends!

BIG PAINTBALL

Prepare to get well and truly splatted in Big Paintball. Run around lots of different levels, pick up a variety of weapons and then blast your opponents with them.

With loads of multicoloured paintballs flying all over the place, you'll need to learn where to find cover on each stage and hide behind it to avoid getting hit.

Big Paintball has lots of cool skins to collect and weapons to unlock, plus there's nothing better than teaming up with your mates to take out another squad.

BLOX FRUITS

In Blox Fruits, players can learn how to become an expert sword fighter. Train really hard and then prepare to battle your enemies.

To survive in this world, you'll also need to collect different fruit. One type heals you, one damages foes and the third transforms you into a beast or animal!

Work your way up through the ranks and take on tough boss characters. Travel across the ocean and find hidden secrets on your quest to be a sword master.

EPIC MINIGAMES

If you're a fan of Nintendo's Mario Party series, then this could be a great Roblox game for you. Try your hand at over 114 different minigames to see which ones you think are the best.

Join your friends online to try out each challenge or play alone to beat each game. Travel across a board game map, unlock pets and become a champion.

Complete each minigame and you'll win coins. These can then be spent on new gear, effects and other cool stuff to make your character even more awesome.

MEGA FUN OBBY

Easily the biggest obby title on Roblox, this game offers players over 2,500 challenging stages to tackle. How quickly can you make it through each course?

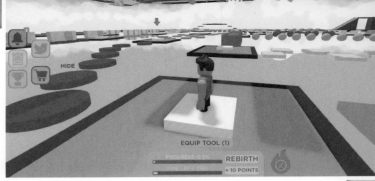

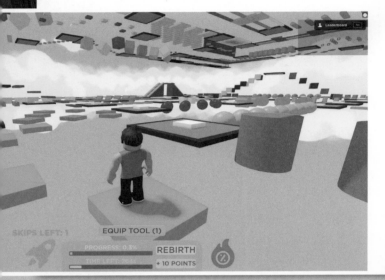

Players begin at the start of each level and then have to run, jump and climb through a series of obstacles to make it all of the way through to the finish line.

There's no time limit on each stage, which is a good thing as rushing can make you fall off. Take your time, beat the level and then move on to the next.

FLOOD ESCAPE 2

When the water level starts rising, you need to start moving! In Flood Escape 2 players have to make their way out of each level without getting totally submerged.

Use all of your parkour skills to run, leap, wall jump, climb and slide to safety. Concentrate on surviving or try to help other players make it out alive.

There are 36 open-themed maps in the game and a variety of liquid-based hazards including rushing water, acid and even red-hot lava!

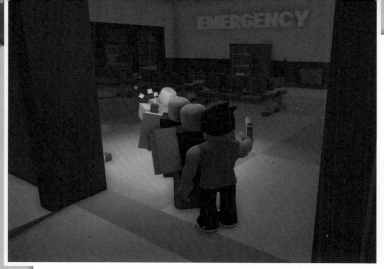

THE APOCALYPSE

Try to survive the end of the world by battling zombies and making it to morning in one piece. If you get bitten, you'll then join the ranks of the undead!

To last out the apocalypse you'll need to learn new skills, board up windows in your building and find food, weapons and supplies.

If you team up with other players, you'll have a much better chance of surviving the night, plus you'll also get to share each other's precious resources.

ANI-BLOX LEGENDS

Play as your favourite Anime characters, fight enemies and team up with others to tackle tough bosses. Build up your powers and take on bigger foes.

Recruit new units to your squad as it begins to grow. As your team's powers grow, so your look will change. Complete each campaign to earn special rewards.

Up to four players can take on Ani-Blox Legends in multiplayer co-op battles. The game is also cross-compatible over consoles and mobile devices.

THE NORMAL ELEVATOR

If you're looking for something a little different to play, then why not step into The Normal Elevator? This is one Roblox title that is completely bonkers!

The great thing about The Normal Elevator is that you never know quite what you'll encounter when those doors slide open. Good luck and try them all!

There are 33 floors to explore, with a different challenge on each one. Some are super-easy, whilst others only last for a second. How many can you beat?

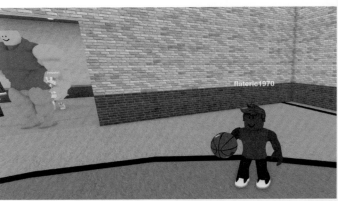

DOOMSPIRE BRICKBATTLE

In this game each player is part of a team that has to guard one of four different coloured towers. The way to win is to defeat all of the other teams in the level.

However, you also have to keep one eye on your own tower. If that gets destroyed by enemy players, then your team will lose the match.

There are lots of different ways to take out other players and destroy towers. Use bombs, rockets, slingshots, paintball guns and more weapons!

ECLIPSIS

Head out on an epic science fiction adventure that's set on a planet hundreds of light-years from planet Earth. Battle to survive on the planet Eclipsis as a hired soldier.

Your mission is to find and secure supplies of a material called Iridium. Your opponents also want to get their hands on it, so you'll have to fight them for it.

Use the Iridium you collect to build up your defences, weapons, gadgets and vehicles. Explore the strange alien world, take out foes and build to survive.

NATURAL DISASTER SURVIVAL

When the natural world starts attacking you, watch out! In this really fun game, you have to survive a series of disasters and be the last person standing.

There are all kinds of tricky elemental dangers to test your dodging abilities to the limit, from tornadoes and flash floods to thunderstorms and meteor showers. Can you survive them all?

The game includes 12 different disasters set across 21 map varieties. This Roblox game is so popular it's actually been visited by players over one billion times!

TOP 10 ROBLOX YOUTUBERS

With millions of players online, Roblox is one of the biggest video games in the world. Check out our list of the top 10 most famous YouTubers making all sorts of videos about the game. How many have you watched?

DANTDM

With more than 22.5 million subscribers and more than 16 billion views, DanTDM is one of the biggest Roblox, Minecraft and Pokémon YouTubers on the planet.

FLAMINGO

Run by USA-based gamer Albert, Flamingo has over 4.56 million subscribers and regularly publishes at least two new video to his channel per day.

DENIS

This is a great gaming channel that has bagged over 8.2 million subscribers so far, with Denis publishing five videos per week that include Roblox.

TOFUU

If you're a fan of both Roblox and Minecraft, then Tofuu's channel is definitely for you. This YouTuber has clocked up over 3.41 million subscribers to date.

SKETCH

Featuring a huge selection of content and four new videos added per week, Sketch has you covered with all sorts of amazing and fun Roblox stuff.

HYPERPLAYS

With entertaining daily video uploads, this YouTube channel run by Dylan is followed by more than 1.65 million Roblox fans from around the world.

POKE

If you want wacky story-based Roblox videos, then be sure to check out Poke. The channel is run by Zack who posts daily to his 4.05 million subscribers.

MOOSECRAFT ROBLOX

You'll laugh yourself silly when you watch Moosecraft Roblox playing the game! This YouTuber has over 850,000 subscribers and his videos are absolutely hilarious.

GAMINGWITHKEV

Another very funny comedy-based Roblox channel, these videos are full of pranks and jokes. Over 5.53 million subscribers regularly check it out.

RADIOJH GAMES

This YouTube channel is run by 15 year-old Audrey, who uploads at least five videos per day for her audience of over 1.2 million subscribers.

BEST SIMULATOR GAMES

In simulator games you can try all sorts of things, from being an animal and working in a laundry to unboxing goodies and eating lots of food.

STRONGMAN SIMULATOR

One of the most popular Roblox games, Strongman Simulator lets your character work out with weights, pump up their muscles and get bigger!

Players start out skinny and are only able to pick up small weights. After plenty of practice you'll be able to lift heavier objects to become stronger.

You'll eventually be able to move massive objects that are way larger than you. Complete quests, earn rewards and train hard to be the best.

BAKERY SIMULATOR

Players can cook up all kinds of tasty treats in Bakery Simulator. There are over 60 cakes, buns, sweets and pastries that can be made in this fun game.

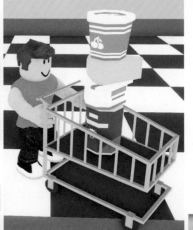

Purchase $38

As you make and sell more items, you'll earn money to decorate your bakery, buy upgrades for your production line and even get cute pets.

The better your bakery does, the more you'll level up and gain access to better equipment and recipes. Do you have what it takes to be a master baker?

EATING SIMULATOR

If making lots of treats sounds like way too much work, then how about eating them? This simulator lets you scoff as much food as you like until you're really huge.

Try to eat a little wisely though, as some food items can be sold instead to upgrade your character. The more you consume, the larger your avatar will become.

The aim of the game is to get as big as you can, but you're up against thousands of other players, so there's always someone out there looking to beat you!

CHAMPION SIMULATOR

Only the very best can be a true champion in this simulator. Punch to gain strength, fight bosses with your friends online or battle other players.

As well as taking on strength challenges, you can also collect various eggs then hatch them into pets. These critters can aid you in battle with special powers.

Champion Simulator has lots to do, from finding gems and upgrading your character to finding new places to visit and discovering secret hidden areas.

SPEEDMAN SIMULATOR

If you're feeling the need for speed, then here's the perfect simulator for you. The aim of this game is to get as fast as you can and beat other players in races.

You may start off quite slow, but with plenty of practice, training and upgrades you'll soon be blasting through every level like greased lightning.

Players can race against their friends, collect pets, unlock all kinds of awesome running shoes, play through regular updates and so much more.

LAUNDRY SIMULATOR

Who knew that cleaning clothes could be so much fun? Own and run your own laundry business by putting lots of items in the washing machine.

The more clothes that you clean, the more money your business will make. You can then use that cash to buy bigger machines, cute pets and cosmetics.

You'll need to move quickly if you want to beat other players though. Keep going and you'll soon have the largest washing machine and laundromat in the whole of the town!

PET SWARM SIMULATOR

This Roblox game was released in 2021 and is loosely based on the world of Pokémon. Travel the world to find the Evil Dark Wizard and save all of the pets.

It's also possible to combine pets to get even rarer creatures, which is a great feature. Be sure to fully explore the map and you might find all kinds of hidden eggs!

Players have to defeat all kinds of enemies on their travels, then feed and hatch their eggs to get rare pets. Build up your collection by beating more tough foes.

ANIMAL SIMULATOR

Not only is this one of the best Roblox games available, it's also visually stunning. Choose from a variety of animals, defeat enemies and level up your character.

There are all kinds of animals in this simulator, including cheetahs, dogs, cats, polar bears and lions. Battle bosses to win treasure and then use loot to buy upgrades.

One really fun aspect of the game is that some animals can actually ride on the back of others. Not always though, so be sure to send a polite request first!

UNBOXING SIMULATOR

Unboxing videos are really popular to watch on YouTube and now you can experience what's it like for yourself in this simple simulator game.

Players get to go off on a box-smashing adventure to see what they might find. Opening boxes reveals special gifts, rare items and even pets to tag along with you.

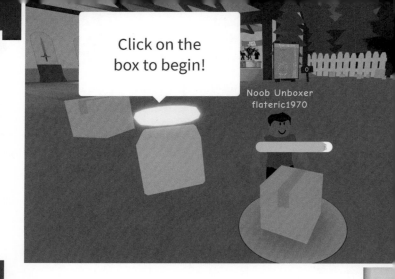

Finding and collecting eggs along the way lets you acquire more powerful pets that will allow you to be the unboxing champion. Go check it out now!

BEE SWARM SIMULATOR

Bees are really amazing creatures. This simulator lets you grow your own swarm, collect pollen and unlock upgrades and become a master at the game.

Players begin the game with just a single bee and have to spend time grinding to level up. There are over 30 bees to collect, items to purchase and ability boosts.

You can also collect the honey that the bees make, meet friendly bears and complete their quests, grow your hive and explore a massive level map.

TOWER DEFENSE SIMULATOR

Another massive Roblox game, Tower Defense Simulator lets you team up with your friends to battle wave after wave of zombies and tough bosses.

By defeating enemies you'll earn coins to buy new towers, build better defences and grab new weapons. The harder the challenge, the bigger the rewards.

Tower Defense Simulator receives plenty of regular updates that always add something new to the game. This is another Roblox game that is great to play with friends.

BUBBLE GUM SIMULATOR

Forget the name of this game, this is one simulator that's really all about pets! Blow bubbles to reach new heights, collect coins and buy even more critters.

You can also use your cash to upgrade your bubbles, buy cosmetics and other items, plus special boosts. There are even limited time events to try out.

Bubble Gum Simulator has had over one billion visits to date and been favourited more than three million times, making it a massively popular Roblox game.

ROBLOX

TOP 10

FACTS

Think you know everything there is to know about the world of Roblox? Check out our top 10 facts on one of the biggest video games ever!

1

ROBLOX CREATOR

Roblox has actually been around since 2006 and was created by David Baszucki, based on a 2D physics simulator that he had made.

2

ORIGINAL NAME

The game was originally called Dynablocks in 2004, but the name was changed as it was thought to be too difficult to pronounce.

3

TIX

You might use Robux to buy items now, but there used to be a second in-game currency that players could use called Tickets or Tix.

4

PURPLE INDY

The fastest-selling item under five seconds in Roblox is this cool skater hat. It's also known as Purple indy.

5

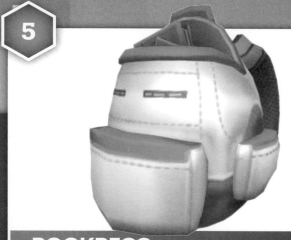

BOOKBEGG

If you buy the Bookbegg accessory from the Avatar Shop, you might be surprised to discover it's actually a hat and not a bag!

6

HOURS OF GAMING

Roblox had over 48.2 million daily active users in 2021. Combined they managed to clock up a staggering 4 billion hours playing all kinds of games.

7

ROBLOX STUDIO

There are more than 50 million community-created games on Roblox. All of the games are created in Roblox Studio, which is an in-game design tool.

8

ADOPT ME!

The most popular game on Roblox in 2021 was Adopt Me! This fun game had over 23.78 billion visits, which is massive!

9

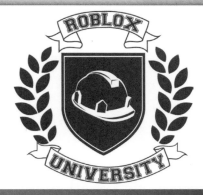

ROBLOX UNIVERSITY

Players that want to get more involved and create their own games can sign up to Roblox University, a series of video guides on YouTube.

10

MILLIONS OF PLAYERS

Roblox has over 202 million monthly active users. In addition, 9.5 million creators also make their own games on the platform for others to play!

BEST TYCOON GAMES

Looking for a different type of Roblox experience? Tycoon Games give players the chance to try their hand at running a business and sometimes make lots of money!

HOSPITAL TYCOON

One of the most popular games on Roblox, Hospital Tycoon lets you plan, build and upgrade a working hospital. Help patients and keep everything ticking over.

Players can unlock new rooms and special equipment for their hospital and figure out exactly what health issues each patient might have, then treat them.

Playing Hospital Tycoon solo is lots of fun, but you can also team up with friends. Fortunately, the game has its own private servers, so the game never gets laggy.

GYM TYCOON

If you're looking for a real workout, try Gym Tycoon from Immortal Games! Pump up your muscles, get fit and earn money running the best gym in town.

The game starts off simply enough. Begin lifting small weights to build yourself up, buy better equipment, train harder and you'll soon be the best on the block.

The more you work out in Gym Tycoon, the bigger and more successful you'll become. You can also fight much stronger players to move up the rankings.

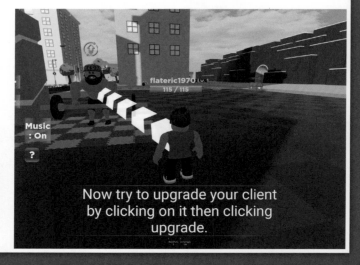

Now try to upgrade your client by clicking on it then clicking upgrade.

RESTAURANT TYCOON 2

Live out your fantasy life being a super-successful chef and restaurant owner! Cook delicious meals, build your kitchen and attract even more customers.

Restaurant Tycoon 2 lets you serve up all sorts of tasty dishes that you have to make yourself. If you don't keep your customers happy, you'll lose money.

The game has all sorts of really cool features, such as a medieval update, lots of different character skins and plenty of regular updates to keep you coming back.

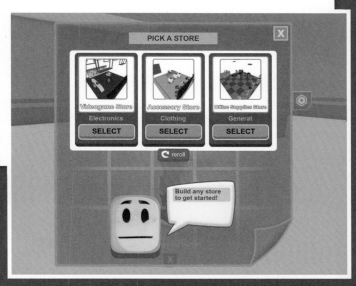

MALL TYCOON

With over 215 million visits, Mall Tycoon is a massive game. Create your very own shopping mall, add all kinds of stores and keep your visitors happy.

It's your job to make the mall run smoothly and to generate as much cash as possible. If you don't please the customers, they'll take their business elsewhere and you'll go bust.

You'll need to decorate your mall and use your money to unlock plenty of cosmetic items. With 12 unique floors, your shopping mall will be huge!

ANIME TYCOON

If you're a fan of all things anime, then this is the Roblox tycoon game for you, as it features fan-favourite characters such as Deku, Goku and Naruto.

Build the best collection of anime characters that you possibly can, then buy and sell others to build up your ever-expanding business empire.

Test out your anime character's powers and weapons in battles with NPCs. You can also unlock exclusive gear, in-game items and cash by joining The Tycoon Games Group.

CLONE TYCOON 2

Unlike other games in this section, Clone Tycoon 2 is a little different. Your goal is to build up a massive cloned army of yourself to send off and fight battles for you.

Level up, unlock all sorts of weapons and cosmetics, upgrade your futuristic base and build a research laboratory to become the king of cloning!

As you progress through the game, you'll be able to buy all sorts of cool new items such as rockets, planes, capes, helmets, new locations and much more.

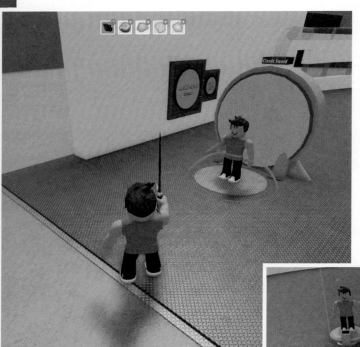

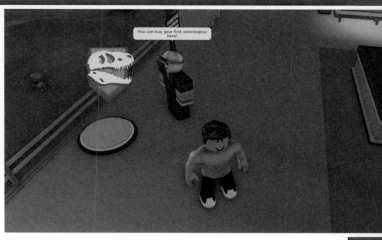

DINO ZOO TYCOON

Fans of all things prehistoric will definitely want to check out this game. In Dino Zoo Tycoon you get to build and run your own awesome dinosaur attraction.

Look after each dinosaur to keep them happy and healthy, but don't forget to keep them far enough away from visitors so that everyone is kept safe.

As your zoo begins to expand, you'll be able to buy even larger dinosaurs to add to your exhibitions. You can also add lots of different rides to your park.

GAME COMPANY TYCOON

How about playing a video game that's all about... making video games! Start programming in your tiny garage to build up your own software company.

If things go well, you'll soon be able to buy an office, hire lots of staff and upgrade your business. The more successful you are, the more money you'll make.

Players can choose whether to make a games company that they enjoy taking care of, or compete against others to reach the top of the global leader boards.

HOUSE TYCOON

Try your hand at seeing what the life of the superrich is like. Build a house and upgrade it, then buy lots of super-expensive sports cars to add to your garage.

Customise your house with a long driveway, water fountains and high-tech remote opening garage doors. Earn lots more money to keep expanding your collection.

There are all sorts of cars to buy in House Tycoon. You can also change the colour of them with a paint job, add accessories and personalise each vehicle.

AIRPORT TYCOON

Running an entire airport might sound like a lot of hard work... and it is! You'll need to be super-organised in this game and ensure that planes are kept flying and landing.

Keep everything ticking over to make money, which can then be pumped into essential upgrades, features, new planes and cosmetic items.

Airport Tycoon gets semi-regular updates to keep things interesting and even lets you add new attractions to your island such as a boardwalk and a ferris wheel.

MY ZOO TYCOON

Take care of lots of cute animals in My Zoo Tycoon. Create and run your own personalised zoo, with over 20 different animal species to choose from.

You'll need to hire zookeepers to look after all of the animals and make sure they're properly looked after. Explore your attraction to unlock new areas.

If you manage to complete activities and minigames dotted around the map, you'll earn cash to buy even more animals and upgrades for your zoo.

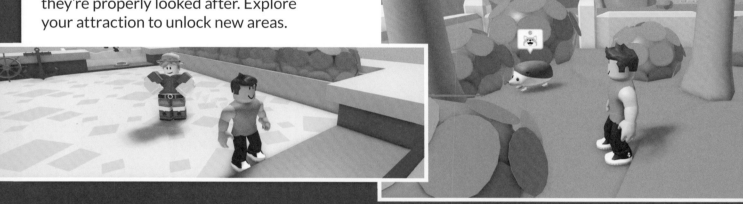

SUPER HERO TYCOON

As well as being a great game for beginners (see page 6), Super Hero Tycoon is also one of the best Roblox roleplaying titles that's been released to date.

Become your favourite superhero and build an epic base. Earn money by undertaking missions and then use your cash to buy even more cool characters.

Super Hero Tycoon has been visited over 1.8 billion times since it was created in 2016. That also makes it one of the top Roblox games ever made!

STAYING SAFE, BEING SOCIAL

FOR PLAYERS

PICKING A USERNAME
NEVER choose a username that has your personal information, such as your real name or birthday.

STAY SECRET
Don't ever give out your real name, address, phone number, or the school you go to. Roblox will never need this info, and neither will anyone else. Roblox has chat software that will automatically try to filter out real-life names for a reason.

STAY IN-GAME
Scammers may ask you to trade money or items outside of the game. That's a good way to lose things. The trading menu in Roblox is designed to protect you, so stick to that and never give anything to people outside the game, no matter how trustworthy they may appear.

DON'T BE AFRAID TO REPORT
Players can easily mute and report inappropriate or abusive chat message, or disturbing content. Just use the Report Abuse system that's located on every single menu and Roblox will be notified and take action as soon as possible.

TELL YOUR PARENTS
Be brave. If someone is bothering you or you saw something you didn't like, tell a parent or guardian. Don't be afraid to say if someone is being inappropriate on Roblox. This game is for everyone and no one should be made to feel unsafe!

"I HEARD ABOUT A ROBUX GENERATOR!"
There are no such thing as Robux Generators – they're made up by scammers to steal money and accounts from players. Don't fall for it. Never trust any websites that aren't official. All official websites end with '.roblox.com'.

FOR PARENTS

BE INVOLVED
The best thing parents can do to make sure their children stay safe playing Roblox is to simply talk to them about the dangers. Make an account for yourself as you make one for your child. You'll even be able to add them as your child on Roblox, allowing you to ensure the social aspects of the game aren't getting in the way of them having fun.

"MY KID IS BEING BULLIED"
If someone is bothering your child, you should report and block them. By clicking on a username you can easily block a user and prevent them from ever contacting your child. By reporting abuse you can make sure that Roblox is aware of the situation.

SAFETY FEATURES
You can sign into your child's account and choose the level of privacy that they have. Make sure you choose the correct date of birth for your child as it sets the default security settings depending on how old they are. You can further modify the settings so that no one can contact your child, or that everyone can. Older players have more options.

MESSAGES AND CHAT
You can easily view your child's private message and chat histories from the main screen. You can also see your child's online friends, the games they've made, and anything they've purchased. If anything looks off, you can then take action.

PROTECTING YOUNGER CHILDREN
While Roblox is tamer than most games, some games feature violence or scary situations. You can go to the Account Restrictions section of your child's account to restrict them from playing anything too intense for their age group.

For many more resources we recommend going to Roblox's official parent's guide at: www.corp.roblox.com/parents There you'll find tutorials for navigating the platform, as well as tips for online safety.